Angel Food
for Thought
BOOK ONE

by Angel Mykel Edwards

PUBLISHED BY
LEAVES OF GOLD CONSULTNG, LLC
P.O. Box 21818 - Detroit, MI 4822
LeavesofGoldConsulting.com
leavesofgold.llc@gmail.com

Copyright (c) 2010 by Angel Mykel Edwards

ALL RIGHTS RESERVED. No part of this book may be reproduced by any mechanical, photographic, or electronic process, or in the form of any audio recording. No part of this book is to be stored in a retrieval system, transmitted or otherwise published or copied for private use without the written permission of the author.

ISBN: 0-9710482-7-4

For more information, contact:
Minister Mary D. Edwards
Leaves of Gold Consulting, LLC
LeavesofGoldConsulting.com
leavesofgold.llc@gmail.com

Book cover and page design by
Shannon Crowley for Treasure Image & Publishing

Photography by William Taylor

Foreword

"Be not forgetful to entertain strangers: For thereby some have entertained angels unawares," Hebrews 13:2 (KJV).

Children must be allowed and given every opportunity to express themselves. When they are permitted to share their feelings, thoughts, hopes, dreams, hurts, and fears, this is a major accomplishment in their personal development. These children are most likely to achieve and obtain more in their lives. They tend to be more grounded emotionally and socially. This builds their self-esteem and confidence. They will be opened to discover more about this world, themselves and others.

You will notice that their personality will emerge. They will be eager to communicate their feelings and thoughts on things they experience in life. Most often, these children will use various mediums or ways to express themselves through artwork, music, writing, and other creative means.

God has truly blessed Angel Mykel Edwards, the author of this book, by giving her the profound gift to write heartwarming and remarkable stories. She is composed, articulate, and an amazing child. She is sensitive to what is happening. She considers challenging and difficult situations. Angel keenly evaluates daily experiences far beyond her young years.

She is constantly searching to find and understand the important lessons to learn from the things she encounters in life. When she discovers it, she wants to share the golden messages or lessons with others. Angel's life is enriched through godly revelations. She has sincere trust in God. She prayerfully reaches out to Him for help and understanding.

In one of her stories, *Dear* MOM: *Why Did You Name Me Angel*, she finds out from her mother that her name, "Angel," means a heavenly messenger. There is no doubt that this young author, Angel Mykel Edwards, is a heavenly messenger!

Her true stories from what she has encountered in her eight years of living, will touch your heart and bring you great joy. Her delightful stories will cause you to wonder how did she even think of that. Some stories will make you laugh and cry.

The Bible says to "train up a child," Clearly you will find parental love and training displayed throughout Angel's life and book. Her dedicated parents are very supportive of her efforts and concerned about her godly upbringing. They have provided for her educational foundation and growth.

Angel is blessed to have grandparents who are great leaders in Michigan. Reverend Eddie K. Edwards and Minister Mary Edwards have devoted their lives to their various ministries and community work. Although her grandfather, Reverend Eddie K. Edwards, the founder of Joy of Jesus Ministry in Detroit has passed, he laid a solid foundation for his children, grandchildren, young people, and families to excel.

His loving and dedicated wife, Minister Mary Edwards, who stood with him as co-founder of Joy of Jesus Ministry, continues to be a powerful leader and productive community worker. In 1999, she founded The Called and Ready Writers, a Christian writing guild. She has helped hundreds of inspiring and advanced writers for years.

However, there is no year as wonderful and glorious as this year, 2010, when Angel Mykel Edwards, their granddaughter came with her parents, Minister Kurk and Michelle Edwards, to the January 2010 opening season meeting to join the writing guild and became an official member. Minister Edwards also had the privilege and blessing of editing and helped compile this first published book for her dearly beloved granddaughter, Angel Mykel Edwards.

The legacy continues! *"...I shall pour out my Spirit upon all flesh; and your sons and daughters shall prophesy... "* Joel 2:23 (KJV).

Let us support the efforts and dreams of our children and their children.

Jesus Christ wants them to come! *"Suffer the little children to come unto me and forbid them not..."* Mark 10:14 (KJV).

Mrs. Wanda J. Burnside, Poet/Author,
President, The Called and Ready Writers

Table of Contents

Dear Mom: Why Did You Name Me Angel?	9
I'm God's Little Angel	11
Dear Mom: If I Be Good, Will I Get Blessed?	13
Dear Mom: I Love You	15
Dear Mom: Why Do I Have Two Fathers?	17
Why You Should Count Your Blessings	19
Why You Should Be A Leader	20
Why The Leaves Fall Off The Trees	22

Why I'm Mad At Eve	23
Who Made God?	25
Prayers Do Come True	26
My Prayers Were Answered	28
How I Kept My Brother Small	30
My Grandpa's Fake Teeth	32
If I Could Turn Into A...	34
Being Safe And Fire Smart Is Important	36
Teasing Molly	38
Selfish Kate	40
Sue's Lesson About Being Wasteful	42
I Love Gymnastics	45
Leaves	47
My Puppy Britten	48
I'm Too Smart To Start Drugs	51
My Valentine Teddy	52

Dear Mom...
Why Did You Name Me Angel?

When I started going to children's church, I found out that God made angels. So, I asked, "Mom, if God made angels, did He make me? "Mom said, "Yes, and that is why I named you Angel because you are a special gift from God."

My mom told me that angels are like messengers and they are around us all the time. So, I asked, "What is a messenger?" My mom replied, "An angel is truly a person who brings a message from God to another person or persons." She told me that in the Bible, Jesus was watched over by angels, and He could call 10,000 angels at one time, if he needed them.

I said, "Mom, do angels work for God to protect us?" Mom said, "Yes." I said, "Mom, I also have an angel doll, and we pray every night.

Our prayer goes like this:
> *Now I lay me down to sleep.*
> *I pray to the Lord my soul to keep.*
> *May angels watch through the night*
> *and keep me in His blessed sight."*

I said, "Mom, angels protect me when I am sleep and all through the day." My grandpa gave me a teddy that is dressed in armor. The teddy's helmet is salvation; his sword is called spirit; his hand shield is faith; his vest is righteousness; and his leg shields are peace. I guess this means that God gives us all of these things to protect us, too. Mom, I really want to work for God. I can be a messenger? I will even work for free. I am one of God's angel, and I need to pray for people and make them laugh and smile.

So you cannot forget to pray every night because God will send an angel to watch over you just like me.

I Am God's Little Angel

One day my brother Kurkie and I went to the doctor's office with my mom. I was five and my brother was three years old. While we were waiting in the crowded office, I noticed a lady across the room talking to someone on the phone. She started to get loud and everyone noticed her. She started to cry, and I felt really bad for the lady. She got off the phone and walked away shouting, "Why me and what am I going to do?"

I felt in my heart God spoke to me and said, "Angel, go and pray for healing and strength and comfort her and I will pour out my blessings." So, I asked my mom if I could pray for her and she said, "Yes."

I was a little scared but God grabbed my hand and led me to the lady. My brother followed me and his face was as sad as mine. I asked her politely, "Excuse me, Miss. Can I pray for you?" She said, "Yes." The nice lady looked me in the eyes with a surprised look on her face, as the tears were falling from her eyes. I put my hand on her back and my little brother put his hand on the other side of the lady. We all put our heads down and I began to pray. I prayed for healing, and strength, and I told her God will bless her today. Kurkie and I gave her a super big hug, and she said, "Thank you so much, sweetie."

I felt really good because I was a good servant and touched that lady's heart. That's why I am God's little Angel.

Dear Mom...
If I Be Good, Will I Get Blessed?

My mom told me that when you are good, God will bless you.

One day Kurkie and I went to the grocery store with our mom and a lady in a wheelchair was trying to reach some milk. I got the milk for the nice lady. I was not expecting the lady to give me a dollar. I just wanted to help, so I told her, "Thank you." I was really happy.

Angel Food for Thought

Another day Kurkie and I were at the Dollar Store with our mom and we were on our best behavior. A lady came up to us and gave me and my brother a dollar. I asked the lady, "Why did you give us a dollar each?" She told my mom that she noticed we were well behaved. I was grateful and told the lady, "Thank you very much." My mom told us that God is watching us all the time, and He will bless us in many ways. I was really surprised.

Finally, my brother and I went to Providence Hospital with Mom because she heard on the news that they were having free heart screenings. So, when we got there, it was a line wrapped around the building. We stood in that line for two hours. I stayed strong and confident that we would get inside of that hospital sometime. There was a couple in front of us and they kept staring and smiling at us the whole time we were standing in line. My mom was next to see the doctor, and I was happy. The couple came out of the room and gave me and my brother $5.00 dollars. My eyes got really big and they told my mom that we were very patient and she trained us well.

I realize that when you are good, God will bless you. Blessings will come in many ways. So, try to be on your best behavior every day. You may not get money, but God will be happy.

Angel Food for Thought

I Love You Mom

*Mom, I love you and I appreciate you.
You are always there for me
Here is a poem that I have written just for you.*

*I love you Mom because you are always there
I love you Mom because you care
You have blessed me with all the clothes I wear
Thank you Mom for my collection
of pet shops and snow globes and my teddy bears*

Angel Food for Thought

I will always love you for everything you do
Especially when you took us to all the Christmas
parties and holiday events too.
I had a blast!
I am growing up so fast.

My brother Kurkie and
I cannot thank you enough
For all the things we have and everything
You have done for us.

That's why I am writing this poem for you
Because it is so true
That you are the best Mom
in the whole universe!

Dear Mom...
Why Do I Have Two Fathers?

ANGEL: *Mom, why do I have two fathers?*

MOM: *What do you mean?*

ANGEL: *My daddy and the Holy Father.*

MOM: *Oh. Here is the story. Listen closely. You see the Holy Father created man. So He created me and you.*

ANGEL: *No. He created Adam and Eve so they could have a baby and start a generation. Oh, I get it.*

MOM: *Now, I hear your brother Kurkie banging on the door. Kurkie, come in and listen. Angel, did your dad start off a generation?*

ANGEL: *Of course not.*

MOM: *Now you see my point.*

ANGEL: *Yes. I do Mom. Dad is not as powerful as God is.*

MOM: *That's right, Angel. Now go to bed. You, too, Kurkie.*

KURKIE: *Aw...Aw...Aw...*

Why You Should Count Your Blessings

Have you ever wondered why you should count your blessings? If you know why, hang in there. If you don't know, I'll tell you now.

When you count your blessings you will get more and more blessings. That sounds exciting to me!

For example, when my mother, my brother Kurkie, and I saw a lady in a wheelchair in the supermarket trying to reach some milk, she couldn't. So my brother and I went over there and helped her get the milk. Then she gave us $1.00 a piece. We said, "Thank you."

This makes me realize if you count your blessings before you go to bed you will get more blessings a day or two later.

Why You Should Be A Leader

You should be a leader because… You do not have to do what other kids tell you to do.

For example, when I was at my old school this girl told me to play with her and I said, " NO!" The game was called spin the bottle. This game dared you to do bad things. If I was not being a leader, I would have got in trouble with God and my lunch aide, and I did not want that to happen!

In addition, on the television show called, "Wizards of Waverly Place," two girls, who were twins, started to follow this girl named Gigi and she was mean to them. They did not know how to tell Gigi that they did not want to be her friend. So, the two girls continued to be Gigi's friend and they got treated horribly.

Leaders come in all shapes and sizes. They can be big, tall, little or small. They can be a boy or a girl and even a mother or father. Leaders want to do the right thing and help people.

Another reason is that everyone looks up to you and appreciates you. They want to be like you and near you all the time. When you are a leader, you will have positive friends. And everyone will count on you to help them achieve things in life. A leader should be a person who never lies and is positive. A leader tries not to hurt other people's feelings. This is what a leader is mostly about and why you should be a leader. Being a leader makes me realize that I can deal with anything. So, that is why you should listen to me and be a leader like me.

Angel Food for Thought

Why The Leaves Fall Off The Trees

Have you ever wondered why the leaves fall off the trees? If you do, hang in there. If you do not, I'm going to tell you right now!

I think that the leaves act really cold, freeze up and fall. For example, in November 2009, I saw some leaves that were so cold that they could not even hold on to the tree branches.

In addition, the leaves are like the tree's blanket. And the leaves hold on to the cold branches until they cannot hold on anymore!

This makes me realize that the leaves have the strength to hold on but eventually fall down. It's not like our blankets. They hold on to us.

Angel Food for Thought

Why I'm Mad At Eve

I'm mad at Eve because she should have never talked to Satan and ate the fruit from the tree. She should have listened to God.

She should have thought about the people in the future. She should have known that God will punish for disobedience. She should not have tried to hide and told God what happened.

God would have forgiven her and we would have had everlasting life. But Jesus had to come and die for her sin. She was being really selfish. She should have thought before she made her action.

God told her more than three times to get away from that tree. But she did not listen. It is all her fault. She should have trusted in God because He is an all-powerful God. She needed to learn how to not be selfish. So do we.

Dear Mom... Who Made God?

Dear Mom, who made God? Did He just appear in the sky? Or did He have another person who created Him? Well, I think God made Himself. God had an idea and that was us!!! and creating animals and nature.

God wanted us to believe in Him. He wanted us to thank Him. But now we are not doing a good job all together. We have people who go to church and praise His Holy Name. On the other hand, we have people that disobey. But kids is not no better. We bully other kids and God is not happy. Our goal in life is to make God happy, yourself happy, and other people happy.

So, please do me a favor. Make God, yourself and everyone else happy.

Prayers Do Come True

One day I prayed to God for a gray cat. I remembered it was in the winter. A couple of days later my dad came home and said, "There is a cat on the porch and he is trying to get in the house." I ran upstairs from the basement and there was a gray cat at my door. So, I let him in the house. This cat was friendly. He ran all over my house and made himself at home. I was excited. My mom said that he must belong to someone and he could stay the night, but I would have to let him out in the morning.

Angel Food for Thought

My brother Kurkie and I played with the gray cat all night. He was so much fun. I could not believe that God answered my prayers even if it was only for one night. This cat was so affectionate. We played ball; we carried him all over the house, and he did not scratch us. The gray cat slept at the foot of my bed.

The next morning I let the gray cat outside and he left. I had a wonderful night with the gray cat. I thanked God for the blessing.

The next summer I found a wild gray kitten across the street from my house. It took me and my mom two months to catch the gray kitten. Eventually, the gray kitten became friendly but he was still too wild to have as a pet. I named him Sammy.

When winter came, my mom decided to take Sammy to the Human Society so Sammy could get adopted and get all of his shots. When I was there, I fell in love with an apricot color cat and begged my mom to adopt him. We adopted him that day and brought him home. My dad named him Garfield because he looks just like Garfield The Cat.

Wow, God is amazing. He let me visit with a gray cat, I found a gray kitten, and adopted a cat that looks just like Garfield the cat. He blessed me with the best cat ever. Thank you God for showing me that prayers do come true.

My Prayers Were Answered

One day I told my dad that I wanted a parakeet bird for my birthday. So, we went to the store and dad bought me a blue and green parakeet with a cage, bird food, and toys. I really loved my bird. I would sing to her, and she would sing to me. My bird would try to get out of her cage. I thought that cage was too small, so mom bought me a bigger cage. My bird still tried to get out of the bigger cage.

I came home from school and ran to my room to see my bird and her head was stuck between the bars and she died. I cried and was really upset. My mom wanted to cheer me up, so we dug a grave in the backyard and placed my bird in the hole. I prayed to God to take care of my bird in heaven.

Later, I asked my mom for another bird and she said, "I cannot afford to buy another bird right now." I said, "Okay mom, I will pray to God to bless me with another bird."

A couple of months later my mom took me to Miss Ross' cookout and she had three birds, two cats, and a dog. She really loved animals. I admired her birds the whole cookout, and I thought about my bird, too.

When it was time to go, I almost made it to the car when Miss Ross said to my mom, "Do you think Angel would like to have my two parakeets?" I yelled, "Yes!" I looked up to God and said, "Thank you God for my blessing. I only asked for one bird and you blessed me with two." My prayers were answered.

> *"Let the words of my mouth and the meditation of my heart be acceptable in Your sight, O Lord, my strength and my redeemer"* (Psalm 19:14).

Angel Food for Thought

How I Kept My Brother Small

When my brother wanted to stay small, we had a talk. And I gave him some good advice.

ANGEL: *"Do you want to stay small?"*

KURKIE: *"Yes."*

ANGEL: *"Do you know how to stay small?"*

KURKIE: *"No."*

ANGEL: *"Don't drink no apple juice. Do you know why?"*

KURKIE: *"No."*

ANGEL: *"Because if you do, you will get bigger, and bigger, and bigger."*

KURKIE: *"What if I drink some orange juice?"*

ANGEL: *"Well, if you drink orange juice, you will get smaller, and smaller, and smaller."*

Angel Food for Thought

He wanted to stay three. So he gave me his apple juice. And I got bigger, and bigger, and bigger. And I will always be bigger than him because I'm his big sister.

That's how I kept my brother small.

My Grandpa's Fake Teeth

One summer day my Mom had to go to work so she dropped off my brother Kurkie and I to my grandpa's house.

When we walked in the door, Grandpa took his fake teeth out and he said, "Do not touch my teeth." He had spit coming out of his mouth.

When he walked out the door, Kurkie put gum in between his teeth.

When Grandpa walked back in and put his teeth in his mouth he goes, "I was not chewing gum and I know who did it. Angel did it. Thank you, Angel."

Angel Food for Thought

I looked at Grandpa like he was crazy and said, "It was a trick."

He walked out the room again and said, "Do not touch my fake teeth." This time Kurkie put a peppermint in Grandpa's fake teeth. Grandpa comes back in again and says, "I was not sucking a peppermint." And he said again, "Thank you for the peppermint," and walked out.

But the third time we put a flower petal in his fake teeth, he came back in the room and put his fake teeth in his mouth and said, "Angel I do not like flower petals."

Kurkie and I just laughed at him.

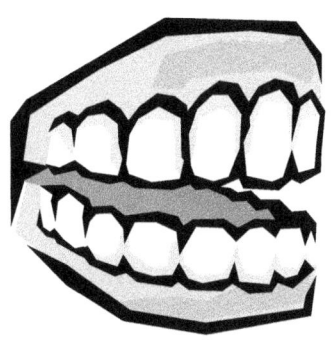

Angel Food for Thought

If I Could Turn Into A...

(Note: This was a class assignment. The class was asked to write about what animal they would be if they could.)

If I could turn into an elephant, I would be big and fat and I will crush you like a bird. Also, I would be free and when I see a hamster I would keep it as my friend. I would be everyone's favorite animal.

I would take over the world, but I mean jungle. I would love to eat grass and plants and suck water up my nose. Alligators would run in terror when they see me coming, because I would step on their little tails. I would make my own grass skirt.

When bunnies come hopping along, I would run them away. I would be seven feet tall and taller than any animal. My other elephant friends' names would be Bumble, Mumble and Crumble. They are sweet but not as sweet as me. This is why I am going to turn into an elephant.

When I read this to my Grammy, she said I should name myself Humble and stay that way. I always listen to my Grammy.

Being Safe and Fire Smart Is Important

Being safe and fire smart is very important in my home. I practice safety every day.

When I go anywhere with my mom, she tells me to look around before we get into the car. She tells me to get in fast and lock the doors. When we get home, I stay in the car and look out while my mom opens the door.

When I was two, Mom told me about the phone number 911. I wanted to practice my new skills, so one day when mom was asleep I called 911 and they came to our house really fast. My mom told the officer that she was sorry I called them. Never call 911 unless it is an EMERGENCY ONLY!!!

She told me never to open the door to strangers or go anywhere with a stranger. A stranger can be a man or a lady. She told me to never give out our personal information to a stranger on the phone.

I saw a tree that had stuffed animals all around. So, I asked my mom, "Why are those stuffed animals around that tree?" Mom said, "Because a child was hit by a car on that corner." My mom taught me how to look both ways before crossing the street.

To stay fire safe you have to stay away from heaters, hot stoves, and do not play with matches or candles because you can get burned. If your clothes catch on fire, you should stop, drop, and roll. If your house is on fire, you must feel the door with the back of your hand before opening it.

Please practice safety every day and have trust and faith in God and He will protect you and your family.

"But let all those rejoice who put their trust in You; Let them ever shout for joy, because You defend them; Let those also who love Your name Be joyful in You. For You, O Lord, will bless the righteous; With favor You will surround him as with a shield"(Ps 5.11-12).

Teasing Molly

Intro: This story is about Angelina and a new girl in her class name Molly. The story can help you understand that teasing can hurt a person's feelings

My name is Angelina and I am in the first grade. Today, a new girl name Molly is in my class. Molly was different from all the other kids. She wore thick glasses and was very quiet, shy and pretty. All the kids in the class thought she was a nerd and teased her. They called her geek and four eyes.

I was very upset when the kids teased Molly. Molly was really sad and started to cry. She hid in the corner at recess and had a sad face for the rest of the day. I really felt bad for Molly. I knew she was feeling sad so I went over to her and cheered her up.

I talked to her and said, "Why did the squirrel want to cross the road so badly?" Molly said, "I don't know." I replied, "Because she saw a squirrel holding a nut on the other side that wants to be your friend." So, the squirrel wanted a friend and took a chance crossing the street and made a new friend.

Molly and I became good friends. Later, the teacher moved me to table four with Molly and I got to know her better. She was a nice and sweet girl. I did not care that she wore glasses and she became my best friend.

Then the next day the kids tried to tease her again and I stood up for Molly. I said, "God created us equal and we are all special in our own way." We are all God's children and He loves us all. If you mess with Molly you will have to mess with me, and I am a child of God." Those kids never messed with Molly again.

"But if you have bitter jealousy (envy) and contention (rivalry, selfish ambition) in your hearts, do not pride yourselves on it and thus be in defiance of {and} false to the Truth" (James 3:14)

Selfish Kate

Intro: This story is about Angelina, and a friend named Kate. This story is about Kate wanting Angelina to be her only friend and that is being selfish.

Kate was in my second grade class and she wanted me to be her only friend. Whenever I would try to play with my other friends, she would get really upset and try to pull me away. When she did that it embarrassed me and upset me. I told Kate that we all can play together as friends. Kate's selfish behavior was not right in the eyes of God. She did not understand at first, and I did not want to be her friend or play with her anymore. She asked me the next day to play with her and I said, "No Thank you!" She got really upset and cried.

God came in my heart and said, "Angelina, Kate does not understand and you need to tell her my word about being unselfish." So I went over and placed my hand on her and said, "Kate the word of God says that your selfish ways are not good in the eyes of God. God wants all His children to love and respect each other. You will always be my friend, and we can have other friends too. "

She stopped crying and she started playing with me and my friends. We all played jump rope and had a good time.

"And the second is like unto it, Thou shalt love thy neighbour as thyself" (Matthew 22:39)

Sue's Lesson About Being Wasteful

Intro: This story is about Sue. She is not aware that she is being wasteful of the things God has blessed us with.

Sue is my neighbor and she lives right next door. Whenever I would go to visit, she would do so many things that my mom told me was being wasteful.

After brushing her teeth, Sue would leave the water running. She was wasting water. She would leave the room with the television and the lights on. She was wasting electricity. She would ask for a lot of food for dinner and would not eat it all. She would throw it away. She was wasting food.

I had a talk with Sue about water and I said, "My mom told me that we need water to drink and clean our bodies. God blessed this earth with plenty of water but not to waste it. "

I had a talk with Sue about electricity, and I said, "My mom told me we need to turn off the television and lights to save energy and save our planet. God created this wonderful planet for us to enjoy and not destroy."

I had a talk with Sue about food and I said, "My mom told me to never waste food. There are children starving and have no food to eat. Never take more than you can eat and do not waste it. God has blessed your family with plenty to eat."

I had a talk with Sue about supplies and I said, "One day I took all the band aids and put them all on my baby doll. I cut my finger and there were no band-aids. I was being wasteful, and I learned my lesson."

I had a talk with Sue about money and I said, "Sue we cannot get mad when our parents tells us they cannot buy us a toy. My mom said, "I have to buy what we need and not always what we want." She said, "Can we eat a toy?" I said, "No Mom, I understand that a toy will not taste too good?"

So finally, I said to Sue, "If you love God, you will not waste the blessings He has given us." Sue said, "I really did not know I was being wasteful and thank you so much for telling me."

"When they were filled, He said to His disciples, "Gather up the leftover fragments so that nothing will be lost."
(John 6:12)

I Love Gymnastics

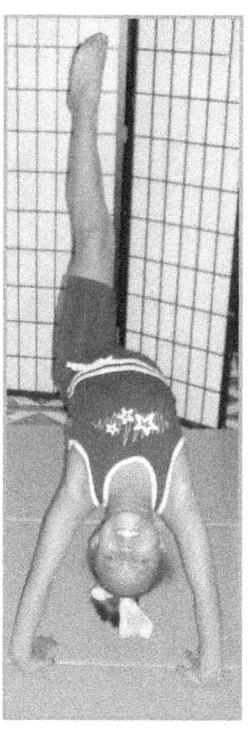

Gymnastics is a sport that brings out my personality. It gives me strength and power. I started when I was only six years old. I know how to do a cartwheel, roundoff, back walkover and forward walkover, back handspring, and a back tuck.

I love gymnastics, and I think it is the best sport in the world. Maybe some day you should try it. The best thing about gymnastics is the coaches. The coaches are very nice. I attend

Angel Food for Thought

Troy Gymnastics in Troy, Michigan. It is almost hard to find it but you know you are there when you see the sign that says "tumbling rocks."

They have all kinds of things you can do there. You can jump in the pit or jump and flip on the trampoline. You can go on the balance beams and the bars.

They have open gym on Saturdays. They have drop in tumbling on Wednesday and it cost $15.00 a person. I always go to drop in tumbling to practice my skills. They have birthday parties there and regular parties. When you become a member, they will send you a list of all the classes.

One day I would like to go to the Olympics to compete.

If I keep practicing and believe and have faith, God will bless me and make my dream come true.

Leaves

FALL, FALL, FALL,
WE WATCH THEM ALL

ME AND MY BROTHER
WATCH THE LEAVES
TURN COLORS

WE PLAY AND PLAY
WE HAVE FUN ALL DAY

THEN IT'S TIME TO GO IN
AND I TAKE OUT THE RECYCLING BIN

I PUT THE BOTTLES IN
AND CALL MY FRIENDS

OFF WE GO TO THE SHOW
WHEN THE LEAVES
TURN TO SNOW

My Puppy Britten

One super fun day, I was playing with my brother Kurkie when something came on my mind. "I want a dog." So I went downstairs and got on the Internet on

Goggle and asked if there was a puppy on sale in Michigan. It pulled up a big picture of a teacup toy poddle. Then my cat Garfield saw the picture of the poddle. He slapped it and the computer felled down. He was jealous. "Oh, Man!" I yelled. But the screen was still on so there was nothing to worry about. So I picked up the computer carefully and went back to what I was doing. Garfield left the room. I didn't care.

So I read the instructions. It said come to Detroit. My mom and little brother Kurkie and I hopped in the car, vroom, and drove off. "WE ARE THERE!" I shouted. We ran to the house. We saw a teacup toy poodle in the window staring out at us. It was cute and tiny. I loved him just looking at him. So we walked up to the door, "Knock, Knock." The owner of the dog opened the door. Her name was Kiss. She asked, "Are you the people I talked to on the phone?" "Yes. We are the people you talked to," we said.

"Are you ready to meet the dog?" She asked. "Yeah!" my brother Kurkie and I screamed.

Kiss took us inside. As soon as we walked in the door, the puppy started to jump on us. "Hey, Kiss," my mom called, "I don't know where the bank is." Kiss said, "I will take you there." All of us hopped in the car. The car started and we drove off.

Angel Food for Thought

We were at the bank. Mom picked up the money and gave it to Kiss. Then we talked about three hours about the three-month-old puppy. She told us that he didn't like to take a bath and when he did, he looked like a pink rat. Glad she told us that ahead of time! Then the time was up and we left. It was almost 9:00 o'clock at night. Then we went to Walgreen's and got a doggy bed.

We named the dog Britten. "We are home. Britten. We got your bed. And here's some toys for you." "Yeah!" Britten barked back. So we put the doggie bed in my bed and Britten got in bed with me. "Goodnight, Britten," I said. Britten barked back, again, "Good night, Angel."

I'm Too Smart To Start Drugs

I'm too smart to start drugs because I have a plan for my life. No one can make me get on drugs. I believe that I'm special in my own way. Drugs cannot stand in my way.

They are bad for my body. They can kill me, and I'm not allowing that to happen. I have been taught and I have seen it happen. It is not going to happen to me because I believe that is what you should believe also.

I trust in you and me so promise to stay off drugs just like I'm going to do.

My Valentine Teddy

One sunny morning I woke up and I said, "It's Valentine's Day!" My mom said that I was right. I ran by the door to see if my dad and grandma were here, but they were not.

I ran in the bathroom where my mom was, and me and my brother Kurkie said, "It's not just Valentine's Day, it is Grandma's birthday." Deep inside I knew I was anxious to give Grandma her birthday gift. I picked it out myself. I knew she was going to love it. It was a book that talks about God's

Greatness, and I got her a poem and it was about God, too.

I ran out the bathroom to the front door and called my dad on my cell phone. I asked, "Where are you Dad. I am waiting?" He said, "I am right here." I saw them turning down the street. I opened the door and they walked in the house. When they were inside the house, I gave them a big hug. Then my dad called, "Where is my Valentine's girl?" I said, "I am right here."

He gave me a bag with a balloon attached. The balloon said "Happy Valentine's Day" and it had a big heart on it. I opened the card and it said, "Daughter, you are one of a kind." The card had a bird and flowers on it. Then I opened the inside of the card and it said, "It means so much to see you spreading your wings, trying new things, and discovering what a unique person you are. It's a special gift to see you grow, to see you dream and I love you more each day, Happy Valentine's Day, Love, Daddy."

I loved the card, it even made me cry.

I looked in the bag and there was a big white teddy bear. It was so cute. The bear had a bow on its neck, and a heart pen on his chest. He was so adorable. I love him and I told my dad I would sleep with him tonight.

Then we all went out for breakfast to celebrate my grandma's birthday. Then we all went home, because I had to run back out to take pictures for the cover of my book. My Valentine's Teddy was with me the whole time. I love my Teddy. I went back home and it was bedtime, so I went to bed with my Valentine Teddy in my arms.

All About Me

My name is Angel Mykel Edwards. I am eight years old, and I would like to become a writer, obstetrician, and an engineer.

My favorite things to do are soccer, gymnastics, and hip-hop dance. My favorite color is pink.

I love GOD, Mom, Dad, and my little brother Kurkie.

I want to thank GOD and the late Rev. Eddie K. Edwards (Papa) who inspired me.

Thank you Minister Mary Edwards (Grammy) for your inspiration and book coaching.

"*I will praise You (God) because I am fearfully & wonderfully made*" Psalm 139:14

This is me with my Grammy, Minister Mary Edwards.

We are wearing black and white (ink and paper), and red hats ("read" all over the world).

Angel Food for Thought

Angel Mykel Edwards
Goals – 2010

1. My book to be published
2. For everyone to know me and buy my books
3. To go on Oprah
4. To learn a lesson from my books
5. To love all of my books

Angel is an excellent reader. She currently is participating in the Southfield Celebrity Reader's Program. Her audience has been second and fifth grade classes at various public schools. She is available to come to your church and share the gifts and talents God has given her.

Contact: Minister Mary D. Edwards
Leaves of Gold Consulting, LLC
(313) 330-4490 ~ leavesofgold.llc@gmail.com
LeavesOfGoldConsulting.com

Angel Food for Thought

ORDER FORM

Angel Food for Thought (Book One)

(NOTE: Prices listed below include 6% sales tax + S/H)

QTY	Description	Price	Total
	Angel Food for Thought	12.75	
	TOTAL ENCLOSED:		

**Discounts available on 10 copies or more.
Call for more information: (313) 330-4490**

Name: _____

Phone: _____

Address: _____

City: _____ State: _____ Zip: _____

Email: _____

Checks should be made payable to and mailed to:
Leaves of Gold Consulting, LLC
P.O. Box 21818 - Detroit, MI 4822
or go to
LeavesOfGoldConsulting.com
to place your order online.

www.ingramcontent.com/pod-product-compliance
Lightning Source LLC
Chambersburg PA
CBHW072034060426
42449CB00010BA/2255